THE STORY OF EASTER

by AILEEN FISHER
illustrated by STEFANO VITALE

HarperCollinsPublishers

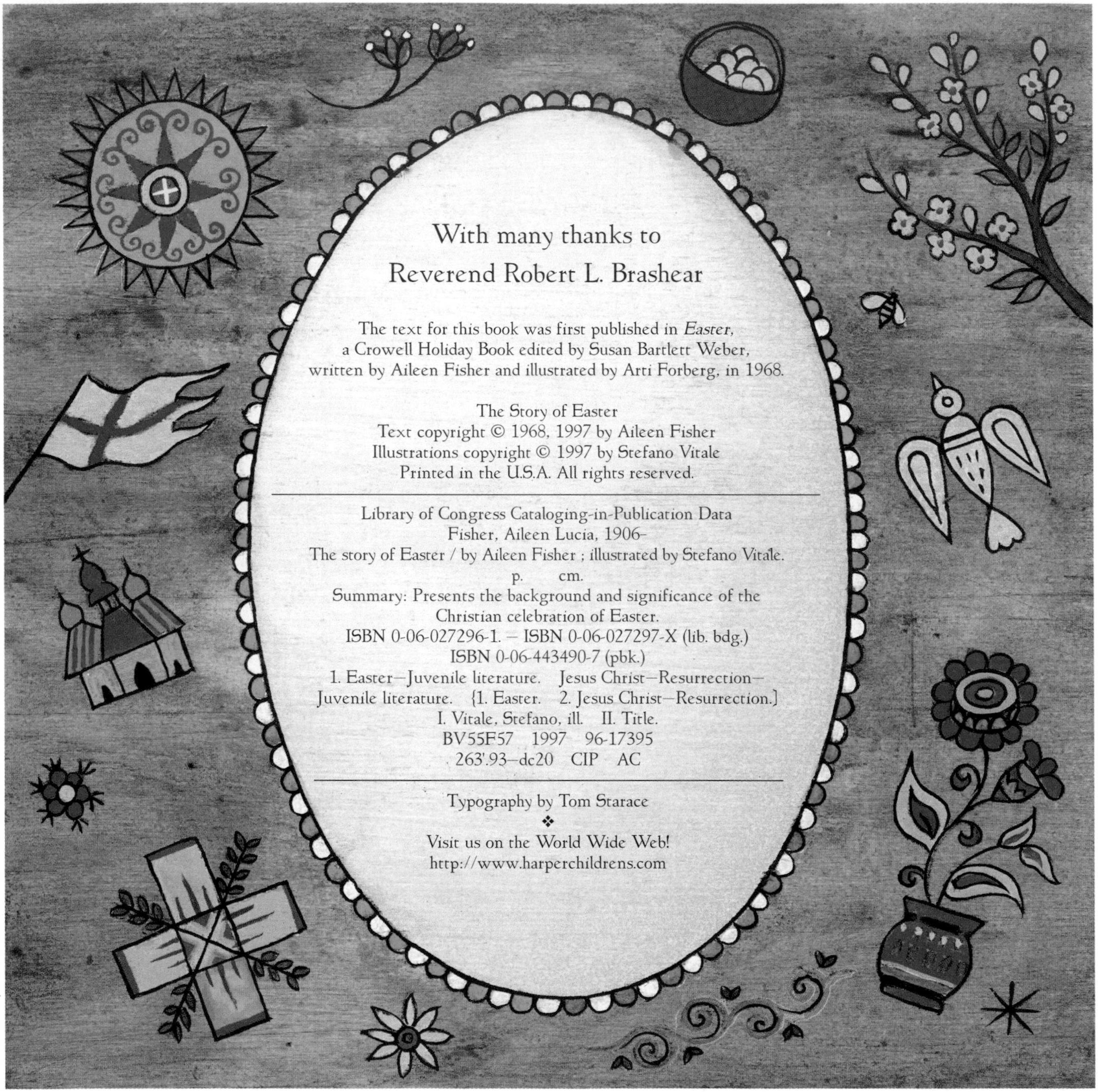

With many thanks to
Reverend Robert L. Brashear

The text for this book was first published in *Easter,*
a Crowell Holiday Book edited by Susan Bartlett Weber,
written by Aileen Fisher and illustrated by Arti Forberg, in 1968.

The Story of Easter

Library of Congress Cataloging-in-Publication Data
Fisher, Aileen Lucia, 1906-
The story of Easter / by Aileen Fisher ; illustrated by Stefano Vitale.
p. cm.
Summary: Presents the background and significance of the
Christian celebration of Easter.
ISBN 0-06-027296-1. — ISBN 0-06-027297-X (lib. bdg.)
ISBN 0-06-443490-7 (pbk.)
1. Easter—Juvenile literature. Jesus Christ—Resurrection—
Juvenile literature. [1. Easter. 2. Jesus Christ—Resurrection.]
I. Vitale, Stefano, ill. II. Title.
BV55F57 1997 96-17395
263'.93—dc20 CIP AC

Typography by Tom Starace

Visit us on the World Wide Web!
http://www.harperchildrens.com

THE STORY OF
EASTER

Easter is a time of rejoicing. It comes in spring, when the cold dark days of winter are over. Birds return to sing. Grass and flowers begin to make a new carpet for the earth.

For Christians, Easter Sunday is the greatest holiday of the year. It is a day of joy. It celebrates the Resurrection of Jesus of Nazareth, who rose from death to new life many years ago.

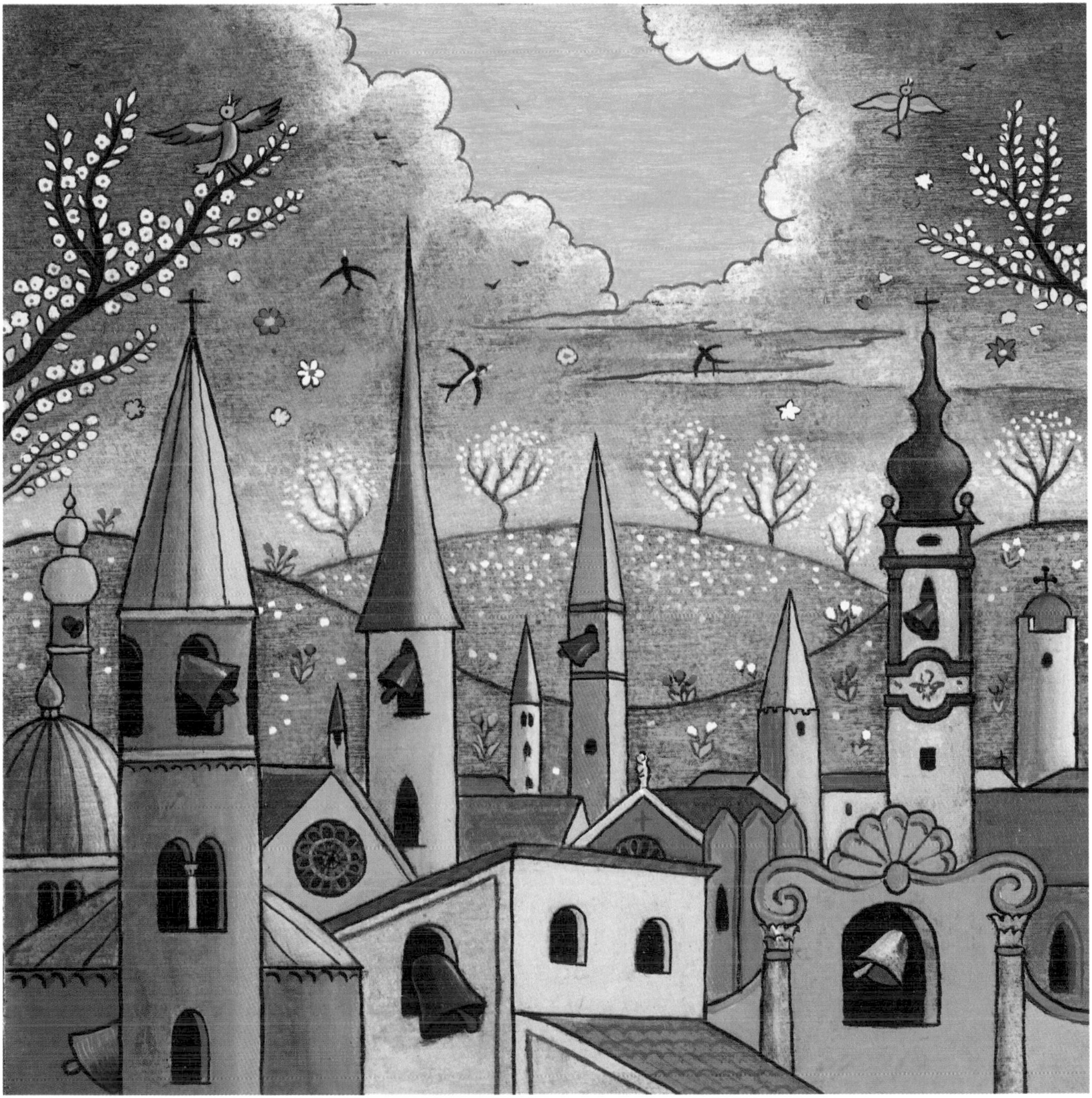

Almost everyone knows something about the life of Jesus.

As a boy he lived in the small town of Nazareth near the Sea of Galilee in what is now northern Israel. When he was about thirty years old, he began teaching and preaching and healing the sick. His fame spread quickly, and soon he had twelve disciples, or followers. They went with Jesus and learned from him as he walked through the countryside talking to the people.

Crowds gathered to hear Jesus preach. Many people began to say that he was the savior, or Messiah, they had long been waiting for.

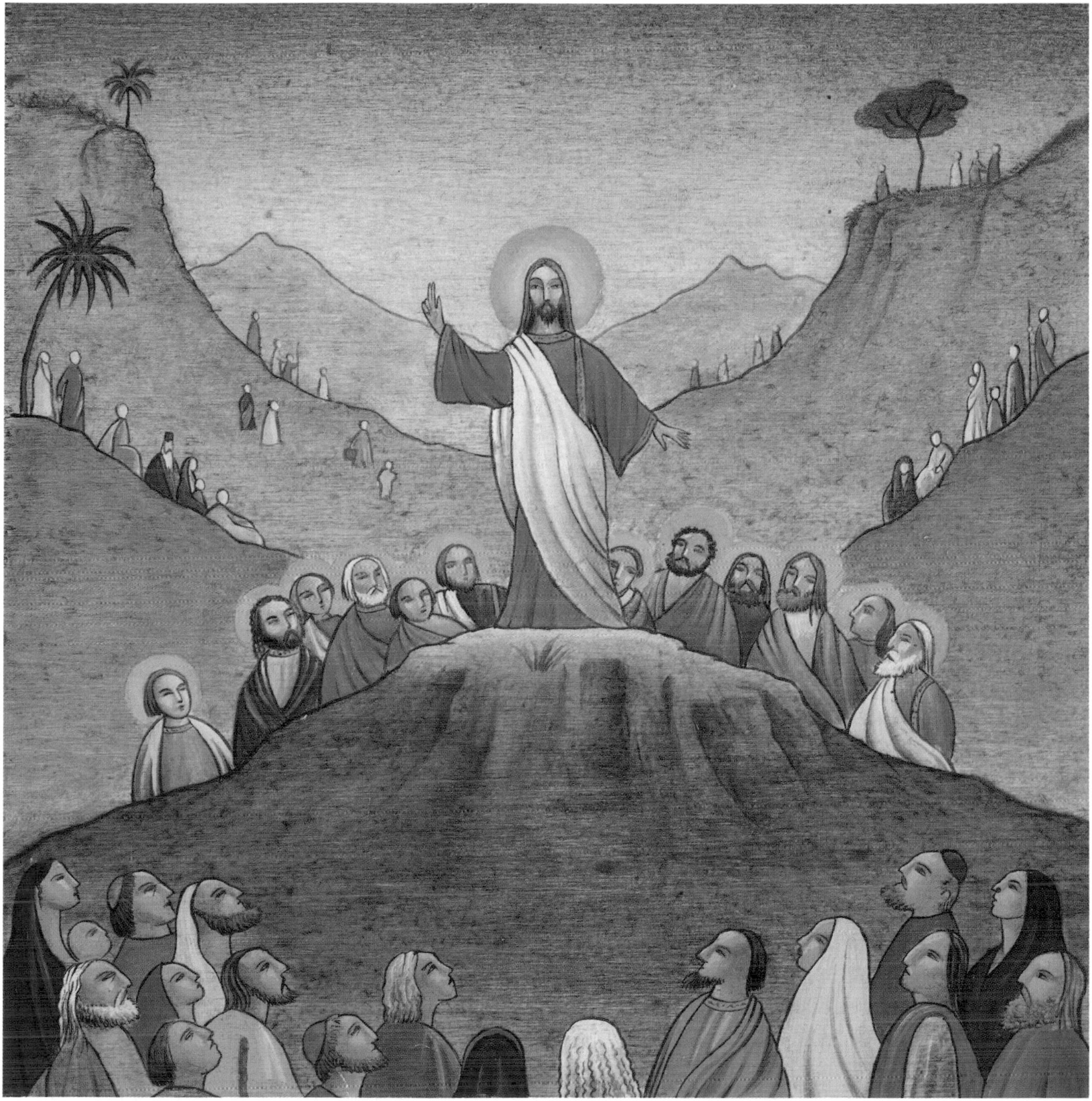

Early one spring Jesus and his disciples walked the long, rough road to Jerusalem to celebrate Passover, the holiday on which Jews celebrate their liberation from slavery in Egypt.

On a mild Sunday morning Jesus rode into Jerusalem on a donkey. People cheered and waved branches of palm trees to welcome him. They spread palm branches before him. In honor of this day Christians celebrate Palm Sunday, the first day of Holy Week. Often palm branches or crosses made of palm leaves are given out at church services.

After that first Palm Sunday, Jesus preached in the outer halls of the great temple at Jerusalem for several days. People crowded around to listen and to praise him. But he had enemies, too. The authorities accused Jesus of breaking laws. They were afraid that he was gaining too much power over the people.

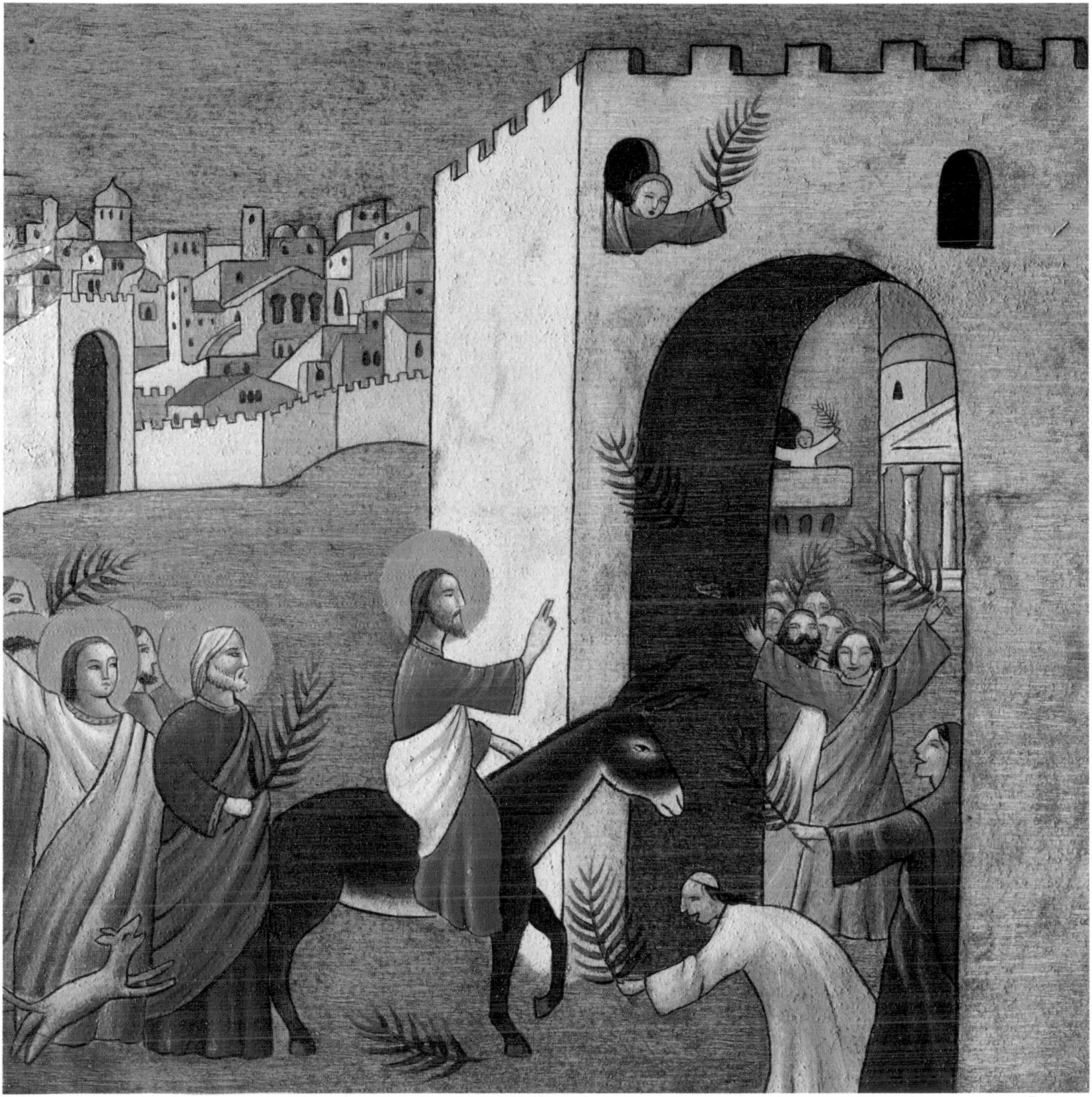

On Thursday evening Jesus ate the Passover supper with his twelve disciples. During the meal he rose from the table, took a basin of water, and began to wash the feet of his disciples. Jesus did this to show that he was willing to be a servant to those who followed him.

We now call this meal the Last Supper and the day Maundy Thursday. For many years the chief ceremony on Maundy Thursday was washing the feet of poor people. Today, people often give Maundy money to the needy as well. In honor of the bread and wine that Jesus and his disciples shared at the Passover meal, many Christians celebrate the Eucharist, or Communion, on Maundy Thursday. This is also a traditional day for First Communions and joining the church.

After washing the feet of his disciples, Jesus led them to a large garden outside the walls of Jerusalem to spend the night. Toward morning, Judas, one of the twelve, led a band of temple guards to the garden. They seized Jesus.

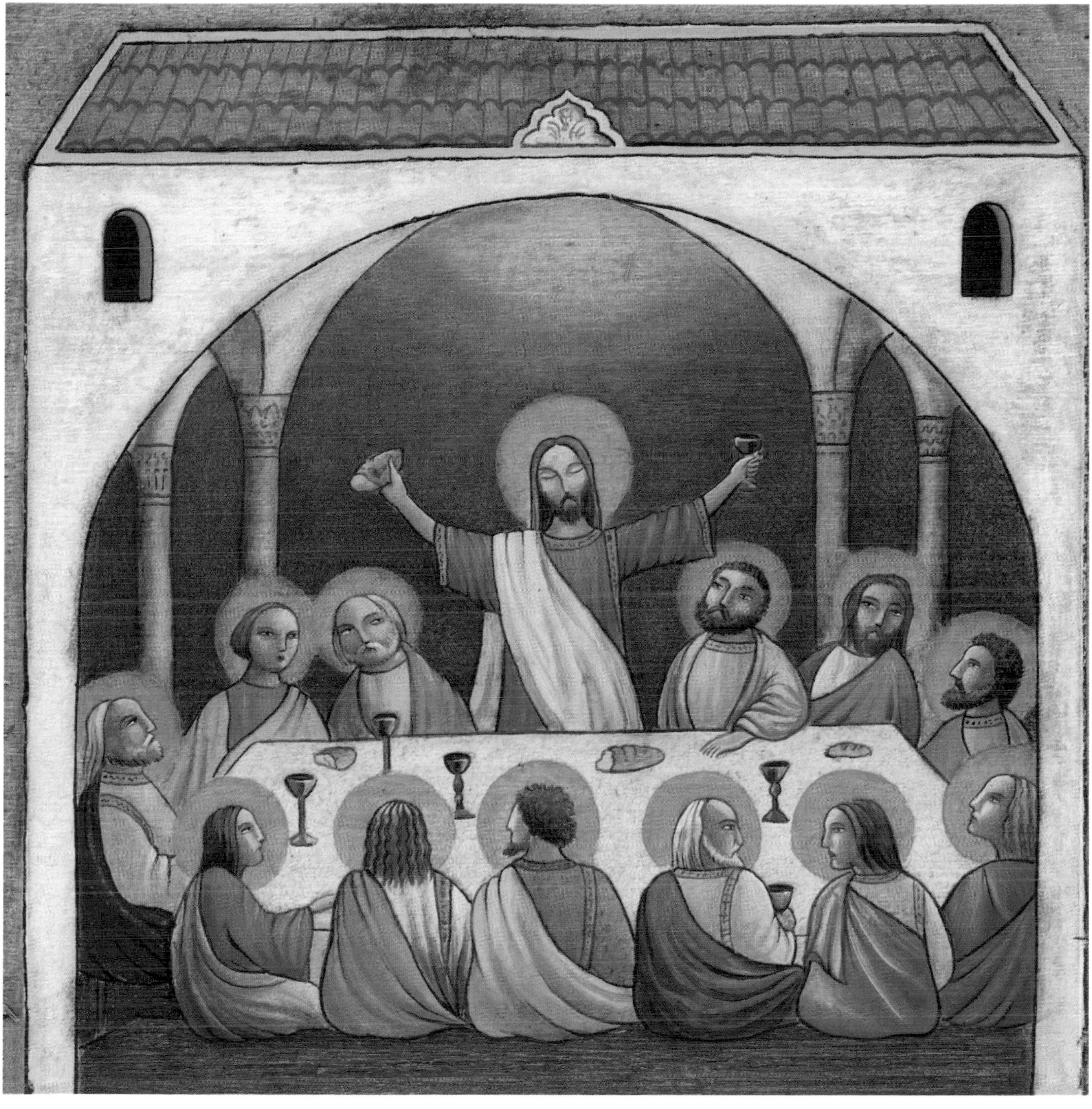

After a hearing the authorities found Jesus guilty of stirring up the people and speaking against the things they held sacred. The Roman rulers sentenced him to death by crucifixion, as was common for political prisoners at that time. So Jesus was taken to a hill outside Jerusalem and nailed to a cross. Because of this, the cross is one of the most important symbols of the Christian religion.

This happened on a Friday morning, a day we now call Good Friday, or God's Friday. For Christians, it is a day of sadness. Many churches hold a service in the afternoon with short sermons about the last words Jesus spoke from the cross.

Before the sun went down on that first Good Friday, friends of Jesus took his lifeless body from the cross. They laid it in a stone tomb and rolled a great stone before the door.

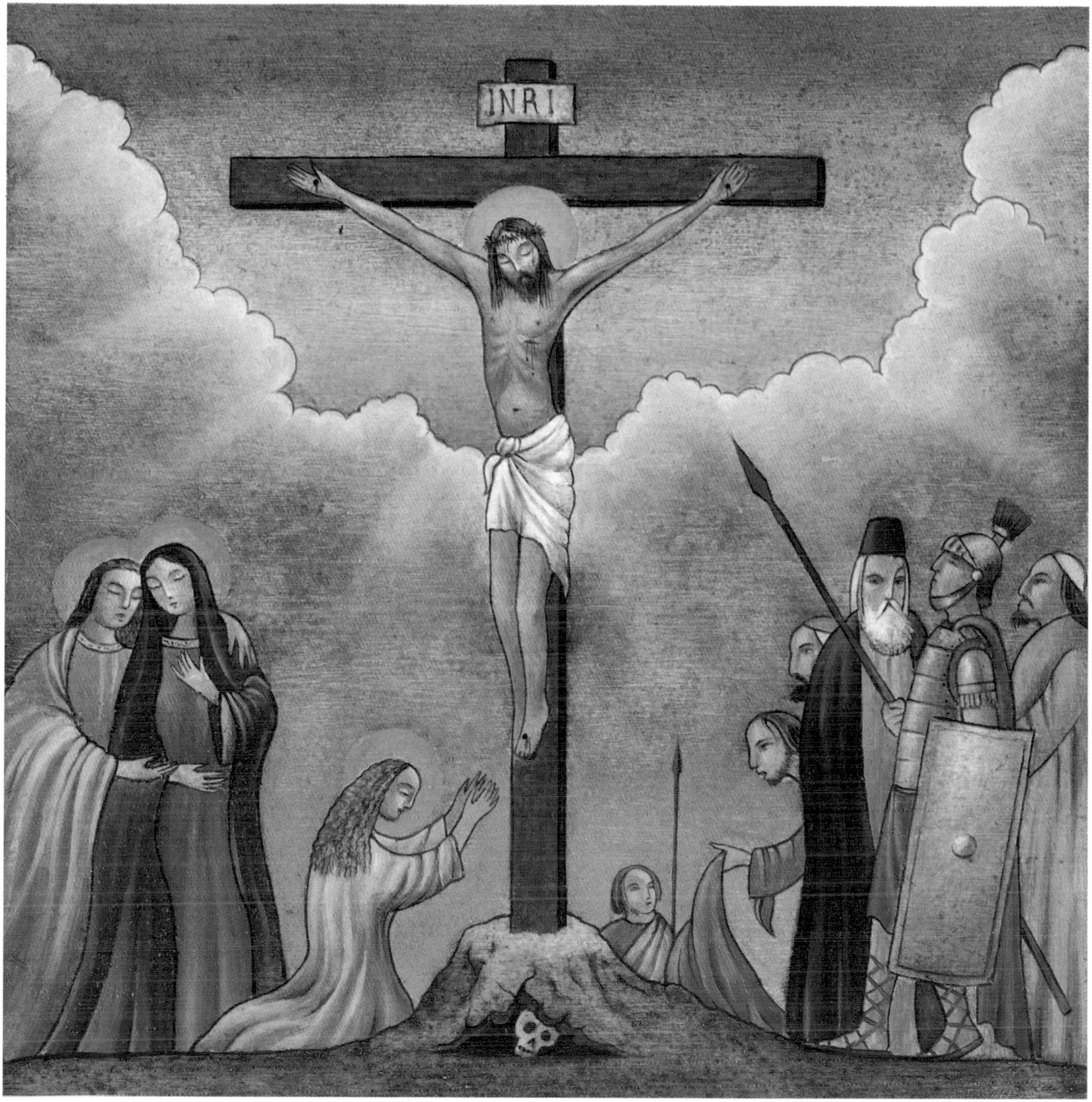
INRI

At sunrise on Sunday morning, Mary Magdalene and two other women went to the tomb. The big stone had been rolled away!

They looked into the tomb and saw a young man dressed in a white robe. "Do not be amazed," he said to them. "Jesus is risen; he is not here."

The women ran to tell the news to the disciples. They remembered then that, while they were still in Galilee, Jesus had told them he would be crucified. And he had also told them, "After three days I will rise again." This was the third day.

On that first Easter Sunday Jesus appeared to the disciples. He told them to go back to Galilee. He said, "Go into all the world and preach the good news."

The disciples understood that Jesus wanted them to spread the good news of his Resurrection and to teach others what he had taught them. And that is how the Christian church was started.

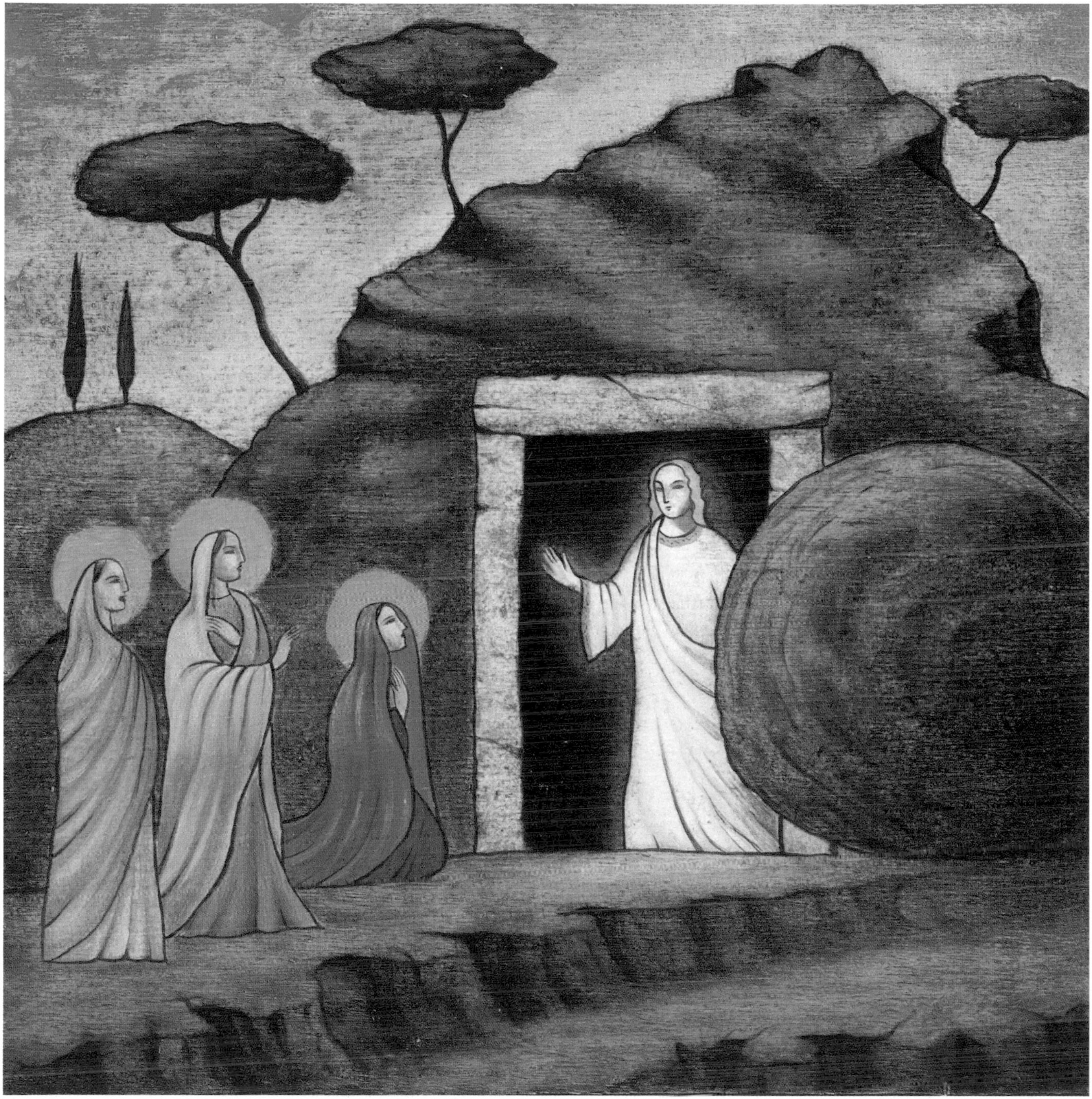

The date of Easter is not the same from year to year. Most people celebrate on the first Sunday after the first full moon in spring. But Orthodox Christians use a different date. They celebrate Easter on the Sunday following Passover.

Long before the celebration of Easter began, people celebrated a spring festival. They danced and gave gifts. They rejoiced over the rebirth of life in the fields and woodlands.

After the Christian religion spread to many lands, the joy of Jesus' Resurrection became mingled with the joy of the spring festival. Both celebrations stood for new life. Both stood for new hope in the hearts of people.

And so it is not strange that many of the customs of the old spring festival became part of our celebration of Easter.

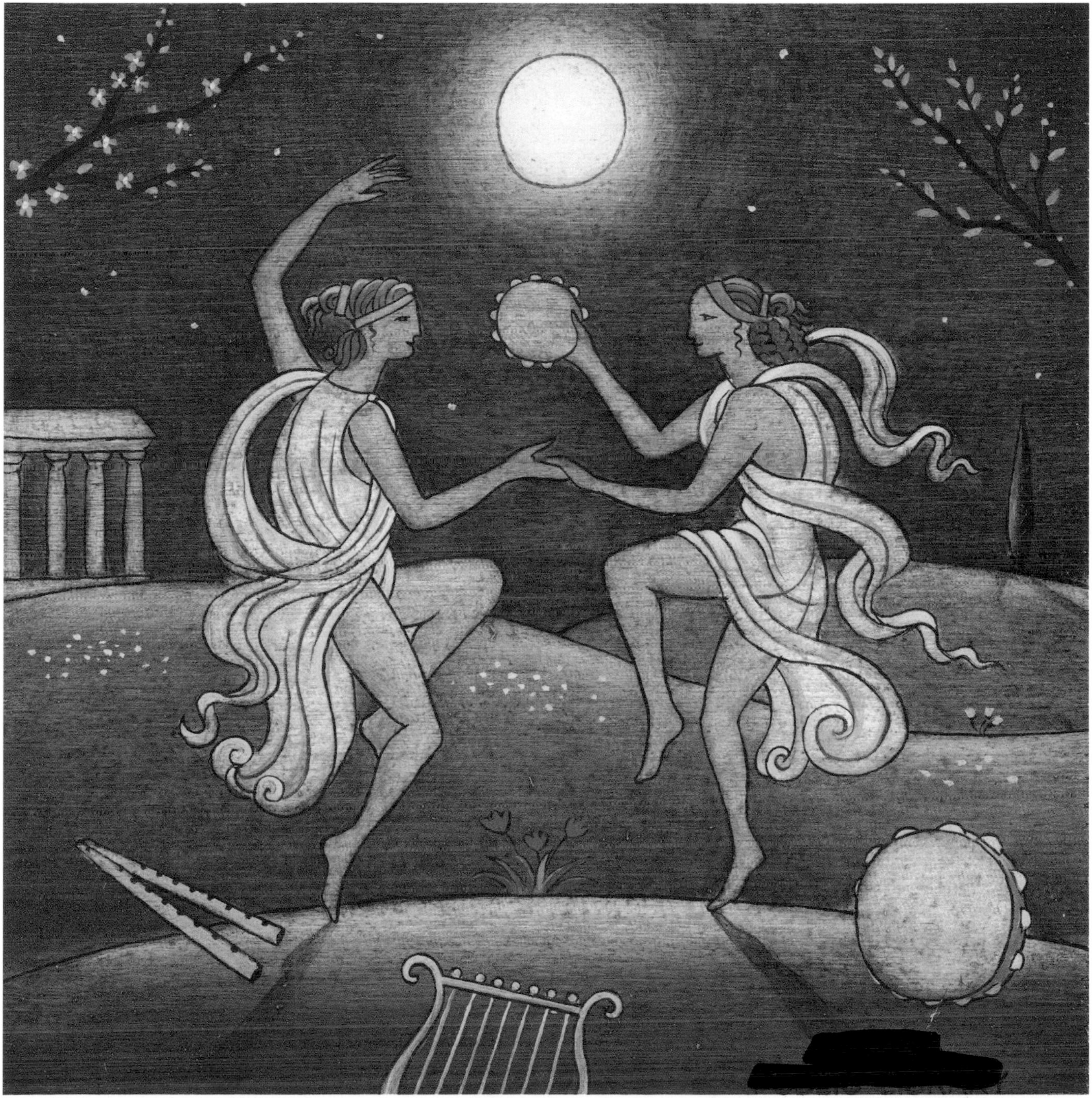
[redacted]

The Easter egg is a good example of a custom that began many thousands of years ago.

For ancient peoples, the symbol of new life was an egg. When the shell broke, new life came into the world. In India and Egypt, people thought that the world began as one huge egg. This world-egg split in two. The upper half became the heavens and the lower half the earth.

For countless years, it was the custom to give eggs as gifts during the spring festival. The ancient Persians and Chinese did it. So did the people of northern Europe during the Middle Ages. The egg is also one of the ritual foods eaten at Passover.

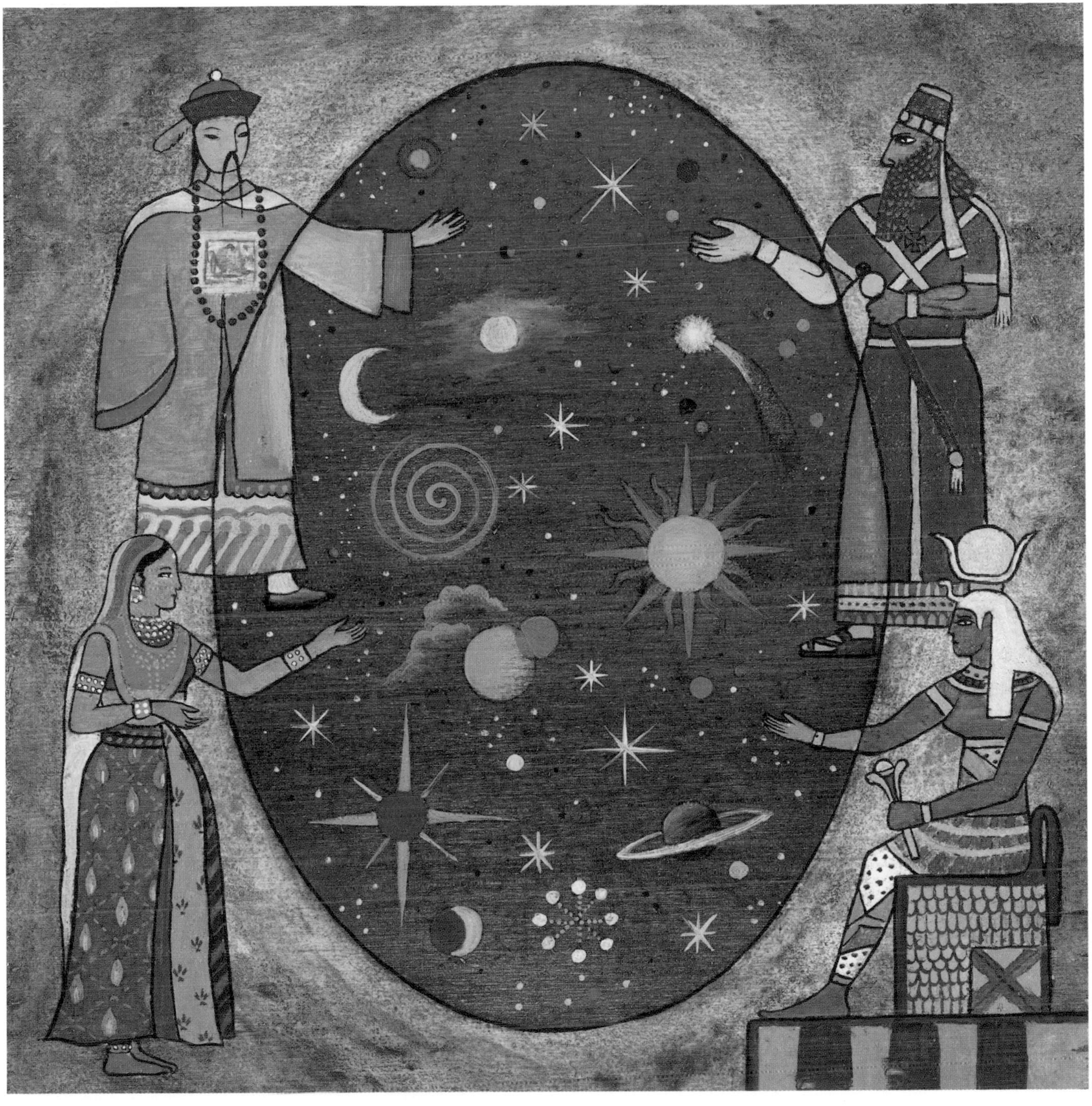

In some countries of Europe decorating eggs has been a great art for many years. In Poland and Ukraine girls and women paint fancy designs on eggs before they are dyed. They paint the designs with beeswax and try to make each one a little different. Flowers stand for love, deer for good health, roosters for wishes that will come true, and the sun for good luck.

After the design is finished, the women dip the eggs in bright dyes. When the dye has dried, the women melt away the wax. The design under the beeswax stays the natural color of the egg.

In Russia artists made beautiful eggs of crystal and gold. Sometimes they decorated them with jewels for the czar and his family. One goldsmith, Carl Peter Fabergé, won worldwide fame for the jeweled Easter eggs he made.

In Greece and Turkey, Sephardic Jews invented a way to dye eggs using onion skins, and this tradition has spread to Latvia and other Eastern European countries.

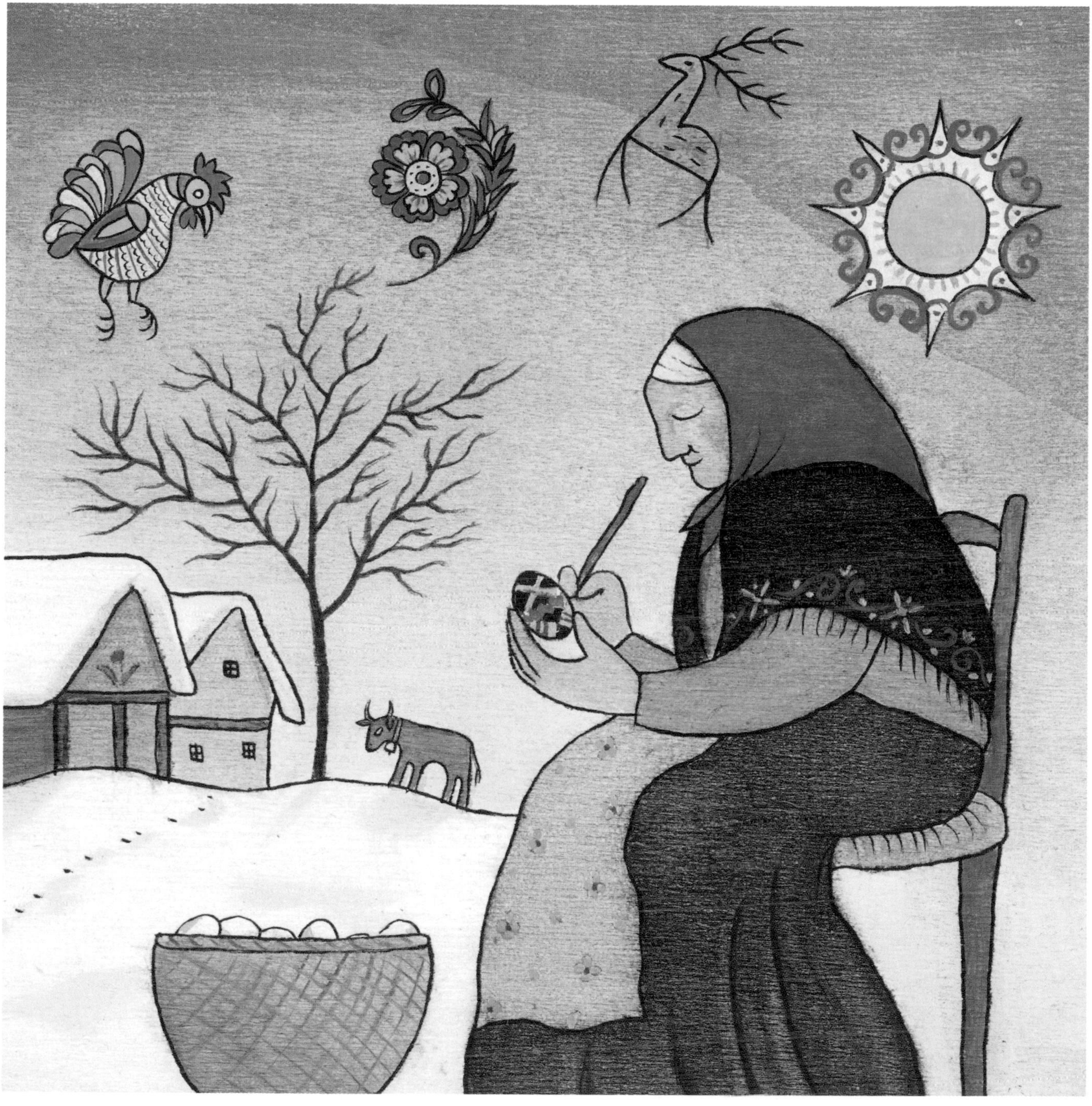

Many of the Easter eggs of Europe have crosses and other religious symbols on them. They carry words or letters that mean "Christ is risen." This is a common greeting during the Easter season, and the traditional response is "Christ is risen indeed."

The Germans were the first to make an Easter-egg tree. Carefully they pricked a hole at each end of an eggshell and blew out the inside of the egg. They colored and decorated the shells and hung them on a tree or bush outdoors. Sometimes they used bright ribbons and tinsel and other decorations on an egg tree indoors. German settlers in Pennsylvania brought the custom of an Easter-egg tree to America.

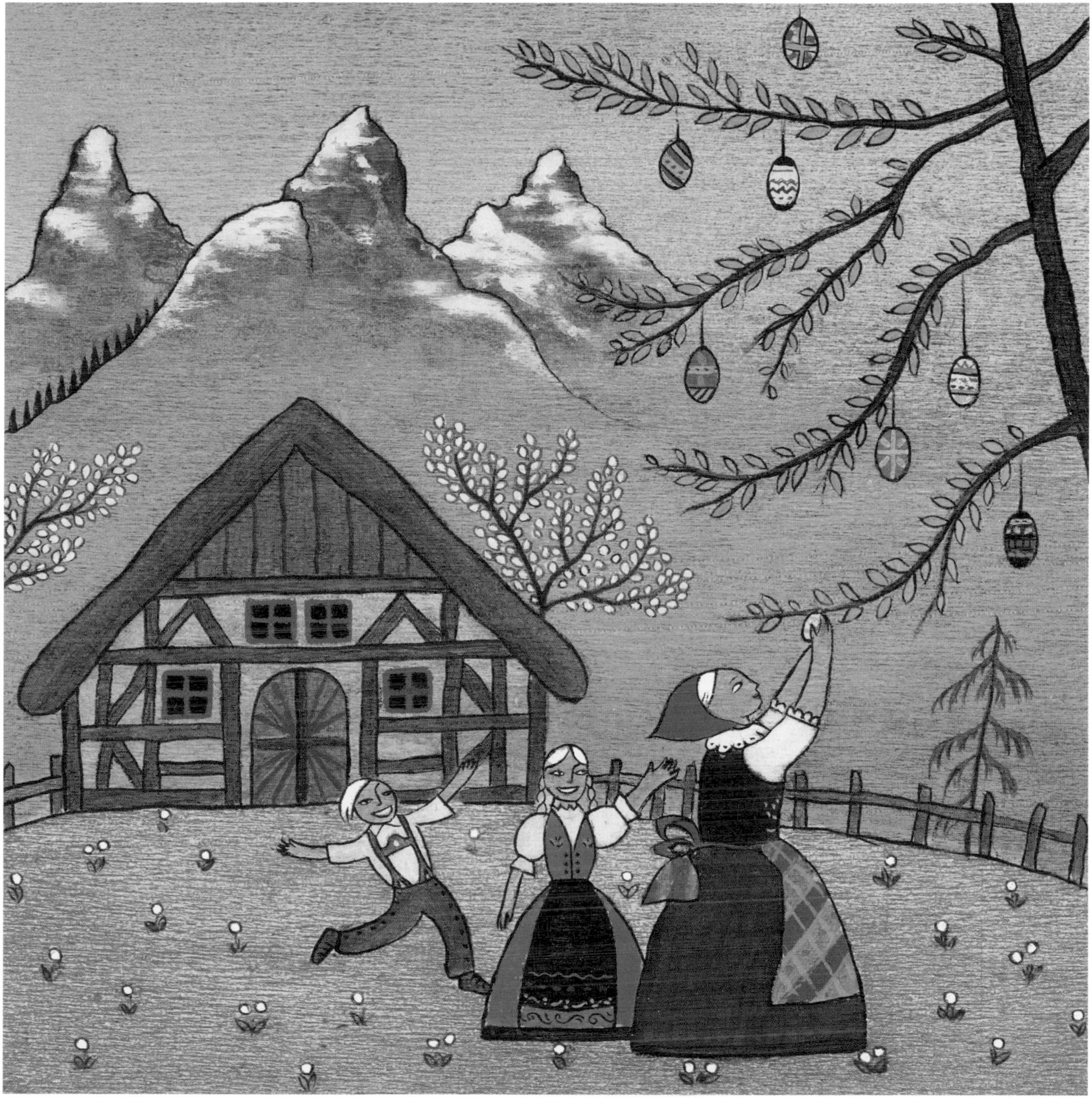

On Easter day there are often egg hunts. Children scurry around to see who can find the most eggs, which have been hidden in the house or in the garden. Sometimes the eggs are real eggs. Sometimes they are brightly colored candy ones, or chocolate eggs, wrapped in foil.

The Easter bunny is supposed to bring the Easter eggs and hide them. He is very shy. He comes at night, and no one ever sees him.

No one knows how the story of the Easter bunny began. But the rabbit is an old, old symbol of the spring festival. It stands for the abundance of new life.

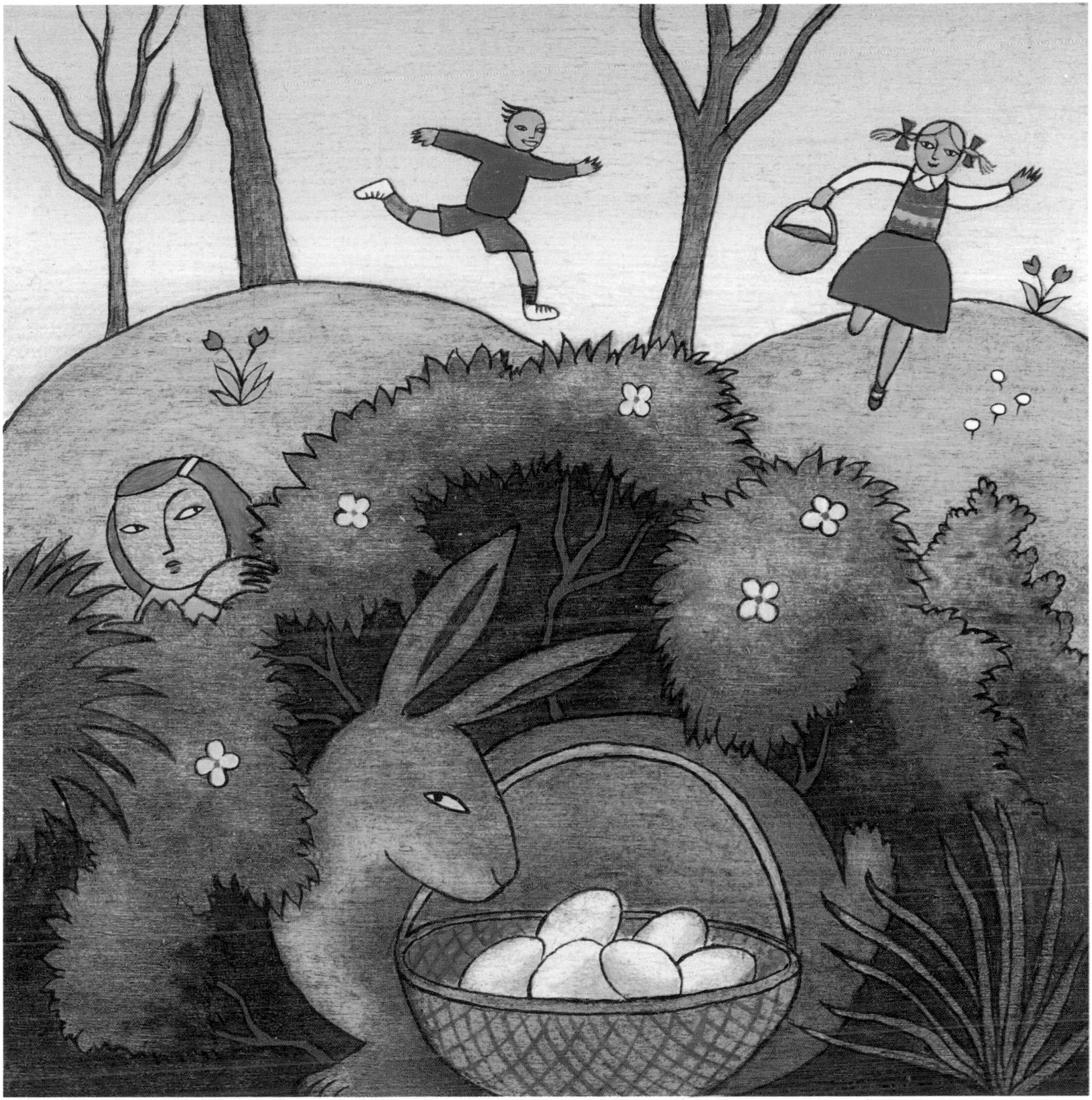

Many of the Easter customs that have come down to us from long ago have changed along the way.

In the days of the early Christians, Easter was the time when new members of the church were baptized. Afterward they put on new white clothes as a sign of their joy. Now people like to wear something new on Easter Sunday.

In Europe, many people carry on the old custom of taking a walk after church on Easter. They walk through the fields to see the flowers and listen to the birds. In New York City this old Easter custom has turned into a fashion parade on Fifth Avenue.

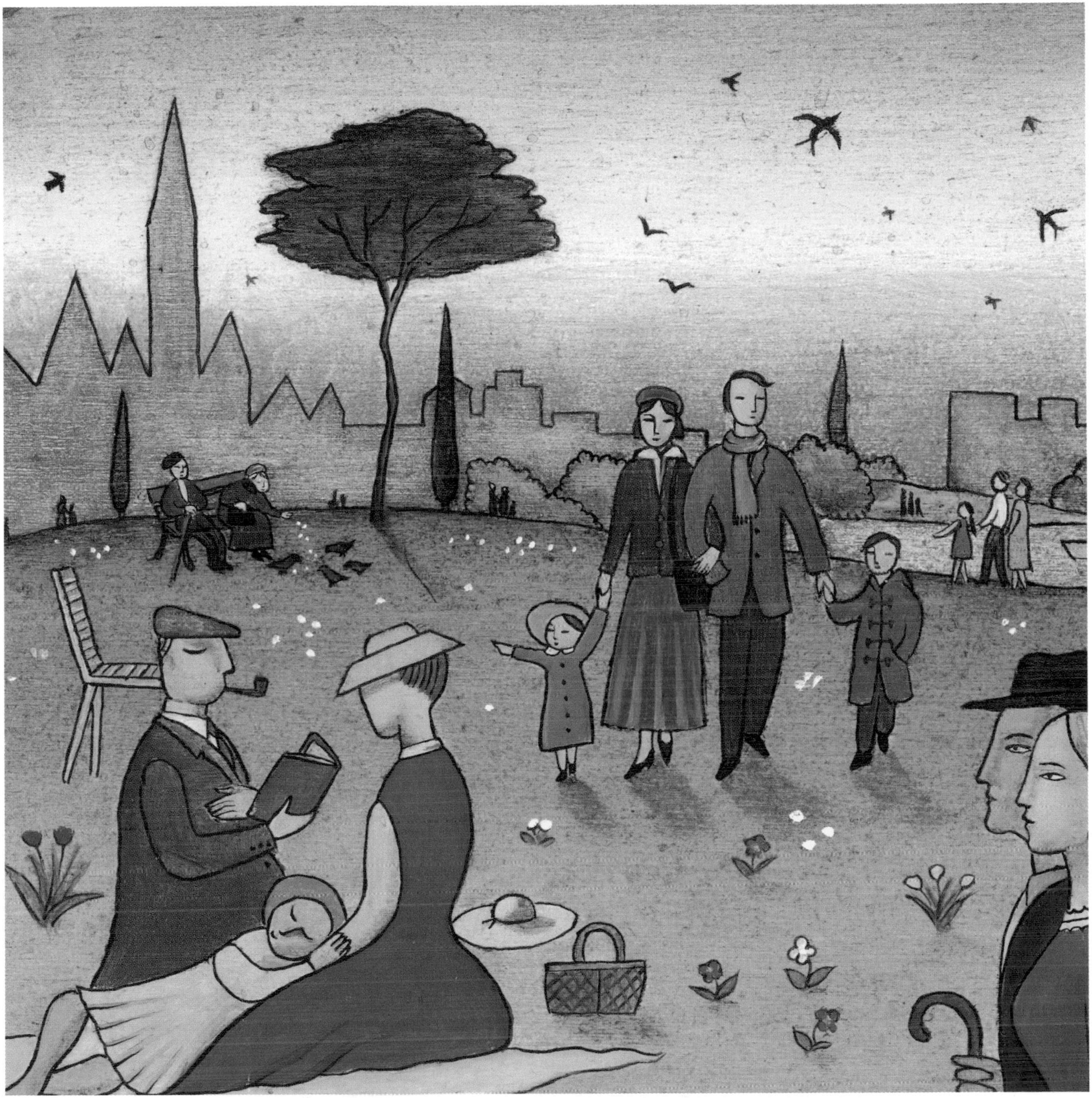

On Easter Sunday millions of Christians attend outdoor services, often on a hill where they can see the sun rise. There is an old saying that the sun dances as it rises on Easter morning.

Inside the churches Easter lilies bloom in front of the altars. People lift up their voices and sing. Not all Christian churches celebrate the Easter season in the same way. But the message of Easter is always the same. It is the joy and celebration of the belief that God's love is stronger than death.

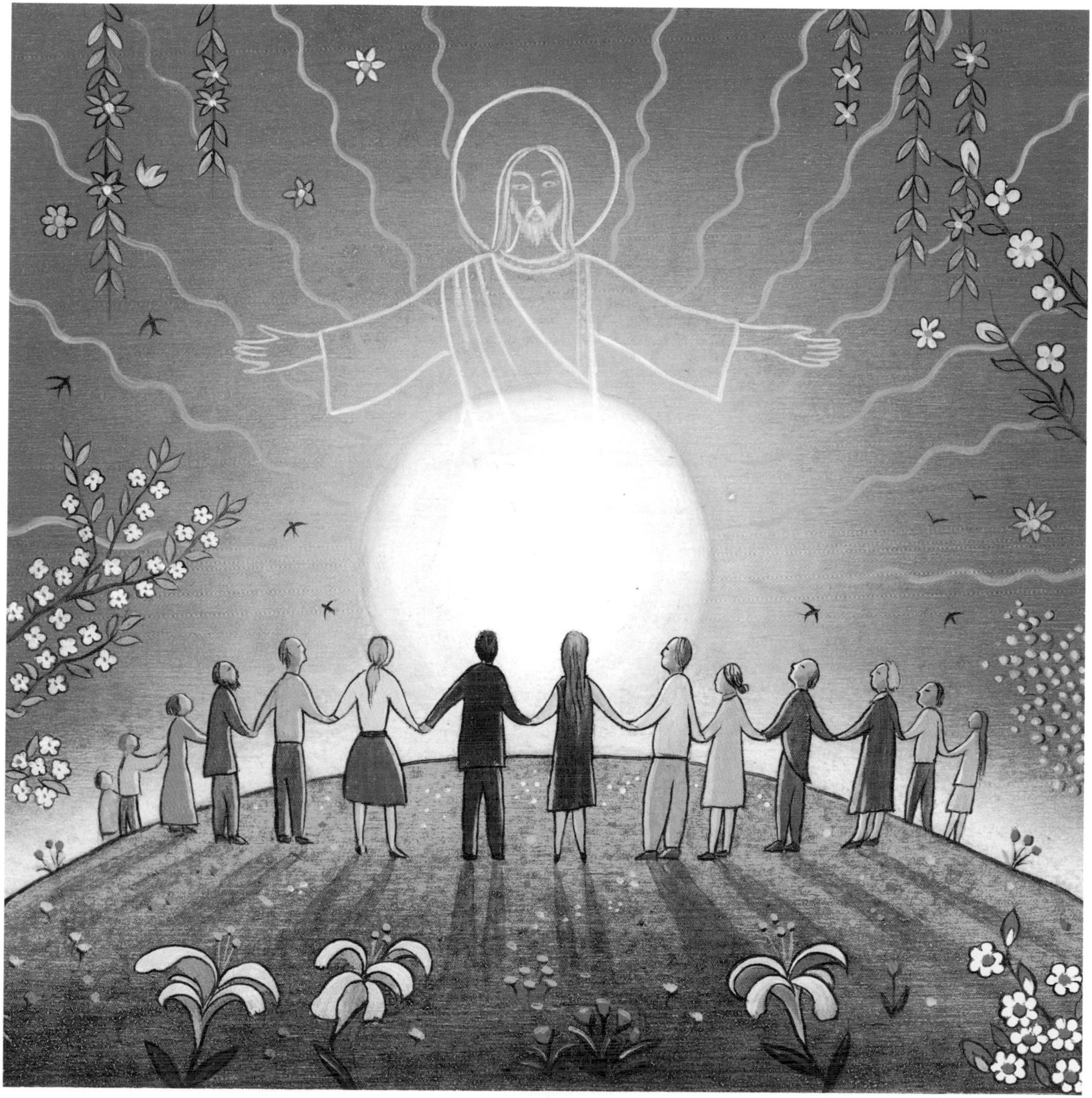

THINGS TO DO AND MAKE AT EASTERTIME

Decorating Easter Eggs

It's fun to dye eggs different colors and then decorate them with ribbon, crayons, stickers, or glitter. You can dye either hard-boiled or blown eggs, depending on how long you want to keep your creations.

WAX OR CRAYON: Dye won't stick to an egg where you draw on it with wax or a crayon. Designs or messages in white crayon or clear wax work well.

BLOCKING: You can also block dye from certain areas of your egg to make patterns. Rubber bands wrapped snugly around an egg before dyeing leave nice stripes. Or you could press a leaf against the egg and tie it on tightly with string.

LAYERING COLORS: You can dye a whole egg one color, or you can use many colors. Try dyeing a whole egg yellow and letting it dry. Then block a section of the egg and put the egg in the blue dye. You should end up with a green egg with a yellow pattern.

Hot Cross Buns

These sweet breakfast rolls are a traditional Easter-morning treat.

Ingredients:

For buns:
4–4 ½ cups flour
1 teaspoon salt
1 teaspoon cinnamon
½ teaspoon nutmeg
½ cup raisins or currants
¾ cup milk
¼ cup butter
6 tablespoons sugar
1 package active dry yeast
⅓ cup lukewarm water (90°–110°F)
2 eggs

Egg wash:
1 egg
1 teaspoon water
pinch salt

Stir together 4 cups flour, salt, cinnamon, and nutmeg in a large bowl. Add the raisins and stir to coat.

In a small saucepan, combine the milk, butter, and sugar, and heat until butter is melted. Allow to cool until just lukewarm. Meanwhile, add the yeast to the warm water and let soften. Beat the eggs well and then add along with the yeast mixture to the milk.

Make a hollow in the dry ingredients and pour in the liquids. Mix to a dough and then turn out onto a well-floured surface and knead 10 minutes or until smooth, adding up to ½ cup more flour if dough is sticky. Place dough in a greased bowl, turning to coat both sides, and cover with greased plastic wrap. Let rise in a warm place until doubled in size, about 1 hour.

Punch down the dough. Divide dough into 12 equal pieces if you want big rolls, or 16 pieces for smaller rolls, and roll them into balls. Place on a well-greased cookie sheet, cover with greased plastic wrap, and let rise again until doubled, about 1 hour.

Preheat the oven to 375°F. Beat together the ingredients of the egg wash and brush gently over the buns with a pastry brush, then bake for 25 to 30 minutes.

When the buns are done, whisk together the following ingredients to make a simple icing:

> 1 cup confectioners' sugar
> 1 tablespoon milk
> ½ teaspoon vanilla or almond extract

Drizzle the icing in the shape of a cross on each bun and serve warm.